D0761131

DESERT

Sean Callery

Consultant: David Burnie

KINGFISHER
NEW YORK

KINGFISHER
LONDON & NEW YORK

Copyright © Kingfisher 2012
Published in the United States by Kingfisher,
175 Fifth Ave., New York, NY 10010
Kingfisher is an imprint of Macmillan Children's Books, London.
All rights reserved.

Distributed in the U.S. and Canada by Macmillan,
175 Fifth Ave., New York, NY 10010

Library of Congress Cataloging-in-Publication data has been applied for.

ISBN: 978-0-7534-6811-1

Kingfisher books are available for special promotions and premiums.
For details contact: Special Markets Department, Macmillan,
175 Fifth Ave., New York, NY 10010.

For more information, please visit www.kingfisherbooks.com

Printed in China
1 3 5 7 9 8 6 4 2
1TR/0312/UTD/WKT/140MA

The publisher would like to thank the following for permission to reproduce their material. Every care has been taken to trace copyright holders. However, if there have been
unintentional omissions or failure to trace copyright holders, we apologize and will, if informed, endeavor to make corrections in any future edition.
Top = t; Bottom = b; Center = c; Left = l; Right = r

All artwork Stuart Jackson-Carter (Peter Kavanagh Art Agency)

Cover main Shutterstock/defpicture; covertl Paul Read/Houston Zoo; covertlc Shutterstock/Henk Bentlage; covertcr Shutterstock/Stefan Redel; covertr; back covertr Shutterstock/
Cre8tives Images; back coverl; back cover Shutterstock/Cre8tives Images; back coverb Shutterstock/picturepartners; and pages 1 Shutterstock/tratong; 2 Shutterstock/wacpan;
3t Shutterstock/James van den Broek; 3b Shutterstock/Rusty Dodson; 4t Shutterstock/Marek R. Swadzba; 4bl Shutterstock/Synchronista; 4br Shutterstock/Dallas Events Inc.; 5tl
Shutterstock/dirkr; 5tr Shutterstock/Vladimir Wrangel; 5bl Naturepl/Peter Blackwell; 5br Shutterstock/Francois Loubser; 6l FLPA/Konrad Wothe/Minden; 6tr Alamy/Julian Money-
Kyrle; 7tl Getty/Digital Vision; 7tr Shutterstock/Chris Fourie; 7ct Alamy/Julian Money-Kyrle; 7c Naturepl/Kim Taylor; 7cr Shutterstock/Arnoud Quanjar; 7br Naturepl/Tony Phelps;
7bc Shutterstock/EcoPrint; 8l Naturepl/Tony Phelps; 8br Naturepl/Ingo Arndt; 9tr Shutterstock/Zavdodskov Anatoly Nikolayevich; 9ct Naturepl/Tony Phelps; 9c Naturepl/Tony
Phelps; 9cb Naturepl/Tony Phelps; 9bl Getty/Animals Animals; 9r Shutterstock/dibrova; 9br Shutterstock/Rusty Dodson; 10l FLPA/Shem Compion; 10tr Paul Reed/Houston
Zoo; 10br Naturepl/Jouan & Ruis; 11tl Getty/Imagebroker; 11tr Shutterstock/ZeroPhanToMs; 11ct Shutterstock/Rusty Dodson; 11c Shutterstock/foto76; 11cb FLPA/Shem
Compion; 11bl Getty/Superstock; 11r Shutterstock/Elbieta Sekowska; 11br Getty/OSF; 12l Getty/OSF; 12tr Getty Images; 12br Getty/Imagebroker; 13tl Getty/Anup Shah; 13tr
Shutterstock/John A. Anderson; 13ct Getty/OSF; 13c Getty/Gallo/Richard du Toit; 13cb Shutterstock/Arnoud Quanjar; 13bl Getty/Eye Ubiquitous; 13r Shutterstock/Susan
Montgomery; 13br Getty/Imagebroker; 14l Getty/Bartomeu Borrell; 14tr Getty/Animals Animals; 14br Alex Wild Photography; 15tl Alex Wild Photography; 15tr Shutterstock/
Brooke Whatnall; 15ct Naturepl/Kim Taylor; 15c Getty/Index Stock Imagery; 15cb Alex Wild Photography; 15r Shutterstock/Joanne Harris and Daniel Bubnich; 15bl PA/Piotr
Nasrecki; 15br Alamy/Chris Grady; 15b Shutterstock/Joanne Harris and Daniel Bubnich; 16l Alamy/Chris Grady; 16br Photoshot/NHPA; 17tl Duncan McCaskill/Wikipedia; 17tr
Shutterstock/Mikhail Nekrasov; 17ct Getty/OSF; 17c Getty/OSF; 17cb FLPA/Martin B. Withers; 17br Getty/OSF; 17bc Shutterstock/Steve Bower; 18l Getty/OSF; 18tr Naturepl/
David Fleetham; 19tl Photoshot/NHPA; 19tr Shutterstock/cellistka; 19ct Getty/Imagebroker; 19c Alamy/David Wall; 19cb Ardea/Auscape; 19r Shutterstock/Robyn Mackenzie;
19br Shutterstock/style-photography.de; 20l Photoshot/John Cancalosi; 21tl Photoshot/John Cancalosi; 21tr Shutterstock/Chekaramit; 21ct Photoshot/John Cancalosi; 21c
Getty/Peter Arnold; 21cb Photoshot/John Cancalosi; 21cr Shutterstock/Mikhail Meinlkov; 21br Getty/Peter Arnold; 21b Shutterstock/Joy Stein; 22l Getty/Peter Arnold; 23tl
Alamy/Joel Sartore/NGIC; 23tr Shutterstock/Joy Stein; 23ct Shutterstock/Caleb Foster; 23c Ardea/John Cancalosi; 23bl Alamy/Cristini Lichti; 23cr Shutterstock/Joy Stein; 23br
Gary Naflis; 25tr Shutterstock/Susan Flashman; 25ct Gary Naflis; 25cb Photoshot/NHPA; 25cr Shutterstock/Bill Florence; 25br FLPA/Konrad Wothe/Minden; 26tr Naturepl/
Phillippe Clement; 26br Auscape; 27l FLPA/Konrad Wothe/Minden; 27t Shutterstock/Tony Cambell; 27tr Shutterstock/pixy; 27ct FLPA/Konrad Wothe/Minden; 27c Getty/Nomad;
27cb Getty Images; 27bl Getty Images; 27cr Shutterstock/picturepartners; 27br Getty/Nomad; 27b Shutterstock/LianeM; 30tl Shutterstock/Piotr Bieniecki; 30tr Shutterstock/
Bretislav Horak; 30bl Shutterstock/Marek R. Swadzba; 30br Shutterstock/Cre8tive Images; 31tl Shutterstock/JuNe74; 31tr Shutterstock/Caitlin Mirra; 31bl Shutterstock/Rusty
Dodson; 31br Shutterstock/Steve Bower; 32tl Shutterstock/Shane Wilson Link; 32br Shutterstock/hagit berkovich

Contents

Introduction

Deserts are large areas of land that get very little rain. Often, they are hot in the day and cold at night. Many desert animals hide under the ground when the sun is up and come out to eat at dusk.

There are fewer plants in the desert than in other habitats, so most animals eat each other in order to live. The list of who eats whom is called a food chain.

The first animal in a food chain eats plants and is known as a consumer. An example is the desert locust, which eats leaves, flowers, stems, fruit, and seeds.

NORTH AMERICA

Food chain 3
Mojave Desert

Equator

SOUTH AMERICA

A food chain starts with a producer: something that makes its own food from the energy of the sun. A cactus is a producer with spines instead of leaves to help it save water.

Smaller, slower consumers are often hunted by bigger creatures or faster ones such as this Namib dune gecko.

This book takes you along three food chains in deserts around the world. You will find out about the life cycles of 11 animals: how they are born, grow, reproduce, and die.

EUROPE

ASIA

AFRICA

Food chain 1 —
Kalahari Desert

Food chain 2 —
Tanami
Desert AUSTRALIA

At the top of a food chain is an animal that is too fast, big, or strong to be attacked such as this black mamba.

Millipede

Millipedes move around through the sandy soil of Africa's Kalahari Desert, seeking leaves and rotting plants to eat. They can grow up to 400 legs, depending on their age.

1 After mating, the female lays about 200 eggs in a nest she has made from dry leaves and dung. She may guard it until her eggs hatch.

2 The eggs lie in the warm soil for a few weeks. When they hatch, the tiny millipedes have seven body segments and three pairs of legs. They grow fast.

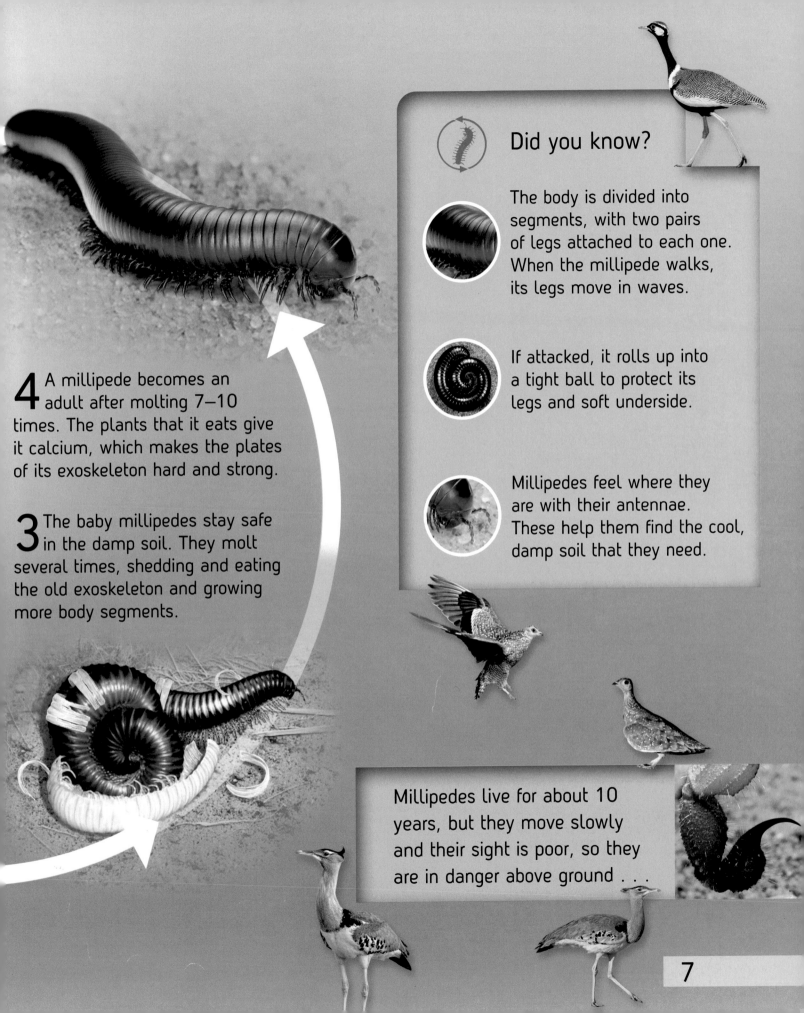

4 A millipede becomes an adult after molting 7–10 times. The plants that it eats give it calcium, which makes the plates of its exoskeleton hard and strong.

3 The baby millipedes stay safe in the damp soil. They molt several times, shedding and eating the old exoskeleton and growing more body segments.

Did you know?

The body is divided into segments, with two pairs of legs attached to each one. When the millipede walks, its legs move in waves.

If attacked, it rolls up into a tight ball to protect its legs and soft underside.

Millipedes feel where they are with their antennae. These help them find the cool, damp soil that they need.

Millipedes live for about 10 years, but they move slowly and their sight is poor, so they are in danger above ground . . .

Scorpion

Scorpions are fighters, with armor to protect themselves and a dangerous stinger for a weapon. They patrol the ground, searching for prey, such as millipedes, insects, and even lizards.

1 The male and female spend hours in a mating dance. After mating, the female gets fat, with about 30 babies growing inside her.

2 After about 5 months, the babies wiggle out of her body. She lets them climb onto her back and carries them around like this.

The stinger carries powerful venom and makes a warning sound when it scrapes against the tail.

The scorpion uses its pincers to hold prey so that it can be stung and killed.

The legs and the underside of the body are covered with hairs. These sense vibrations from creatures moving nearby.

4 The young leave their mother after 1—3 weeks when they have shed their skin for the first time. They molt another five times or more as they grow into adults.

3 The tiny, pale young hold onto their mother with their pincers. The remains of the yolk inside their bodies keeps them alive.

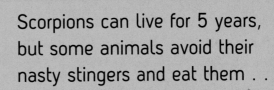
Scorpions can live for 5 years, but some animals avoid their nasty stingers and eat them . . .

Meerkat

Meerkats live and hunt in gangs. They rest at night in underground burrows linked by many tunnels. During the day, they feed together, mostly on insects. They will also fight and eat scorpions.

1 Meerkats can mate three times per year. The female gives birth to three pups in the burrow. They do not open their eyes for at least 10 days and their ears are folded back.

2 The pups leave the safety of the burrow after 3 weeks, watched by a "babysitter."

Did you know?

The long, strong, curved claws are well shaped for digging burrows, scratching for insects, and climbing trees.

Meerkats take turns to stand as a lookout. They have special barks for threats such as eagles and snakes.

Their neat, small ears fold back when they are digging to stop soil from getting inside.

4 Hunting training begins when pups are 1 month old. They are able to take care of themselves completely after about a year.

3 The pups are looked after by the entire gang. Even females that are not yet mothers can produce milk to feed them. The pups will suckle for about 8 weeks.

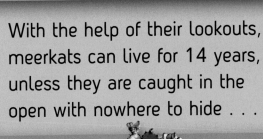

With the help of their lookouts, meerkats can live for 14 years, unless they are caught in the open with nowhere to hide . . .

Jackal

Jackals are fierce, fast hunters that eat anything they can catch, including meerkats and larger prey. They also scavenge dead animals, eating flesh that would otherwise lie and rot.

1 Jackals mate for life. They dig a den 3–7 feet (1–2 meters) deep or take over one dug by other animals.

2 Nine weeks after mating, the female, or vixen, gives birth to 3–6 pups. They have no teeth, and their eyes are closed for 10 days. One pup often bullies the others to give it their food.

Did you know?

Jackals have large, pointed ears that help them hear other animals far away and even under the ground.

Sharp, curved canine teeth at the front of the mouth are for piercing and gripping prey. Behind them are molars that grind and crush food.

Their long legs and large feet allow jackals to jog at 10 mi. (16km) an hour for a long time to chase down their prey.

4 Young jackals can take care of themselves after 6—8 months. They will all leave their parents to find their own territories.

3 The pups suckle milk for 4 months and also eat food choked up, or regurgitated, by their parents. They learn to hunt by playing chase and tug-of-war.

Jackals can live for about 8 years. Adults are fast and strong, so few other animals dare to attack them.

Termite

Termites live in massive, tall mounds in the Tanami Desert, in Australia. The mounds have many underground tunnels and can be home to millions of the insects. Termites mostly eat dead plants.

1 A queen termite can lay thousands of eggs every day. She gets so big that she can hardly move. Worker termites feed her and take away the eggs that she lays.

2 After a month, the eggs hatch into nymphs. The colony feeds them for another month and helps them molt by biting off their outer skin as they grow.

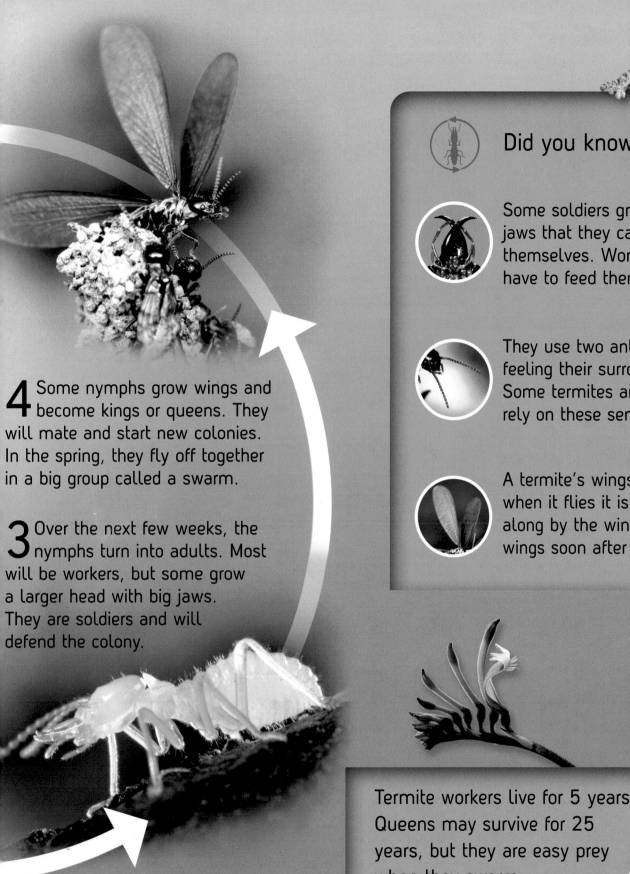

4 Some nymphs grow wings and become kings or queens. They will mate and start new colonies. In the spring, they fly off together in a big group called a swarm.

3 Over the next few weeks, the nymphs turn into adults. Most will be workers, but some grow a larger head with big jaws. They are soldiers and will defend the colony.

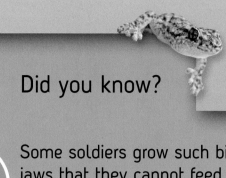

Did you know?

Some soldiers grow such big jaws that they cannot feed themselves. Worker termites have to feed them.

They use two antennae for feeling their surroundings. Some termites are blind and rely on these sensors to "see."

A termite's wings are weak, so when it flies it is mostly blown along by the wind. It sheds its wings soon after landing.

Termite workers live for 5 years. Queens may survive for 25 years, but they are easy prey when they swarm . . .

Red-capped robin

The red-capped robin lives in dry areas of Australia. It feeds mainly on the ground, pecking up spiders, beetles, and other insects such as termites. Males have brightly colored plumage, but the females' feathers are dull.

1 Robins pair up to mate. The male brings food to the female while she builds a cup-shaped nest. The nest is covered with moss that is tied in place with spiderwebs.

2 The female may have three broods per year. She lays 2–3 eggs and keeps them warm until they hatch after 2 weeks. The chicks' eyes are closed.

4 The chicks fly off to find their own territories when they are about 6 weeks old. Adults mostly live alone. Males get their bright plumage after a year.

3 After a week, the chicks open their eyes, start to stretch their wings, and in one more week they can fly. The parents feed them for another 3 weeks.

Did you know?

The male's bright plumage comes from the red insects and berries that it eats. The color helps it attract a mate.

Three toes point forward and one backward on each foot to grip branches. When the bird sleeps, its leg muscles tighten to stop it from falling off.

A red-capped robin is a songbird. It has many calls for attracting a mate and for scaring rival birds away from its territory.

These birds can live for 5 years, unless a big bully with a forked tongue finds their eggs . . .

Perentie

The perentie is a 7-foot (2-meter)-long lizard that will eat anything it can sniff out, from birds' eggs to a small kangaroo. It swims, climbs trees, and runs on two or four legs.

1 The female checks the soil carefully to find a place that will be warm enough to keep her eggs alive. Then she digs a burrow.

2 She lays 6–10 eggs in the burrow and covers them up. Some mothers lay them near, or even in, a termite mound so that the new babies can eat the insects.

4 Perenties are very good at climbing trees to grab eggs from birds' nests. They sometimes snatch up the birds as well!

3 In about 3 months, the first hatchling cuts open its shell. It does this with a piece of hardened skin, called an egg tooth. This will fall off later.

Did you know?

The perentie has a forked tongue like a snake. It flicks in and out as the lizard searches for smells in the air.

Each foot has five long, sharp claws that are good for grabbing prey and digging burrows.

The perentie swings its tail to hit attackers and also uses it for balance when it stands on its back legs.

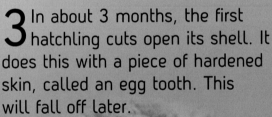

A perentie may live for 20 years in the desert, because no other creature threatens it once it is an adult.

Cactus mouse

Cactus mice dig burrows in the sandy ground of the Mojave Desert, in California. They climb up cacti and other plants to escape from predators, and hide, almost asleep, from the worst of the summer heat.

1 Three weeks after mating, the female produces a litter of up to four babies. They are born blind and helpless.

2 The babies' ears unfold within a day but their eyes do not open for at least 2 weeks.

4 Cactus mice survive on very little water in the hot, dry desert. They get most of the liquid they need from the fruit and plants they eat.

3 They feed on their mother's milk for more than a month. Females are able to mate at 2 months old and can have a litter three or four times a year.

Did you know?

Its very long tail helps the mouse balance as it runs, climbs plants, and scampers over rocks.

When they are excited, cactus mice thump their front feet on the ground to make a drumming noise.

Their ears are large and their hearing is very good, which is helpful because they are most active at night.

Cactus mice can live for a year if they stay away from big, hairy monsters . . .

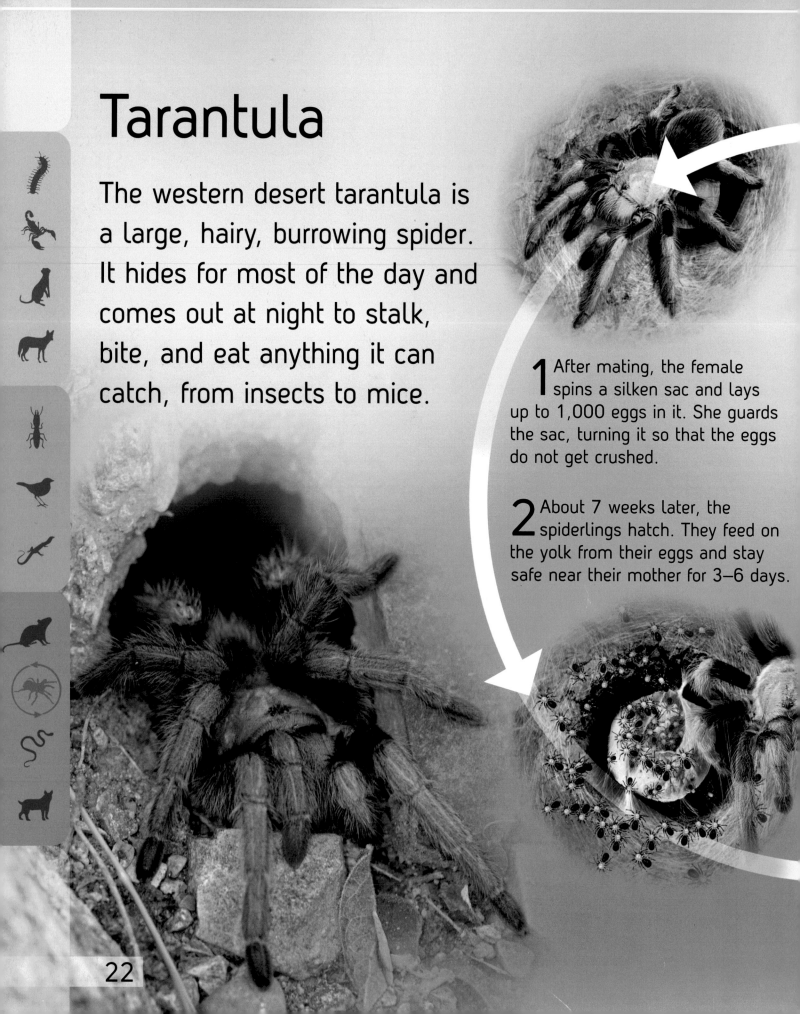

Tarantula

The western desert tarantula is a large, hairy, burrowing spider. It hides for most of the day and comes out at night to stalk, bite, and eat anything it can catch, from insects to mice.

1 After mating, the female spins a silken sac and lays up to 1,000 eggs in it. She guards the sac, turning it so that the eggs do not get crushed.

2 About 7 weeks later, the spiderlings hatch. They feed on the yolk from their eggs and stay safe near their mother for 3—6 days.

4 The tarantula injects its prey with venom, killing it and turning its insides into a soup. Then it sucks the liquid out with its strawlike mouth.

3 Then the young leave to find their own burrows. They shed their hard exoskeletons several times as their bodies grow.

Did you know?

 The spider's fangs turn down to strike and fold away like a penknife blade when they are not needed.

 The spider senses the world through the thousands of hairs covering its body. The hairs are also itchy to predators.

 Each leg has two or three claws at the end that the spider uses to grip surfaces when it climbs.

Tarantulas live for about 10 years. They hide from predators during the day, but danger can slither across the sand . . .

Shovel-nosed snake

When it is getting dark, western shovel-nosed snakes leave their underground burrows and wiggle their bodies to "swim" across the desert sand. They eat spiders and insects.

1 After mating, the female digs a burrow and lays 2—4 eggs. The best burrow is one that gets a lot of sunshine so that the soil is warm. She leaves the eggs there.

2 It is not known for certain, but it may take 3 months for the babies to grow big enough to break out of their shells. Hatchling snakes look like adults with larger heads.

4 Like many other desert reptiles, shovel-nosed snakes survive the winter months by hibernating deep in their burrows where it is a little warmer than outside.

3 The hatchlings quickly learn how to feed and defend themselves. Their main weapon is their tiny teeth, which they use to grab prey before swallowing it whole.

Did you know?

The snake is perfectly shaped for burrowing. It even has flaps on its nostrils to keep out the sand that it tunnels through.

If it is disturbed and cannot escape, the snake curls into a ball. It might also hide its head in its coils.

Shovel-nosed snakes are not venomous, but they have stripes like coral snakes, which are venomous. This puts off predators.

Snakes can live for 20 years if they stay away from sharp teeth and claws in the dark . . .

Bobcat

The bobcat, or lynx, lives in many habitats, including deserts. It is a tough cat that uses its senses of sight, smell, and hearing to hunt down its prey, which ranges from deer and snakes to insects.

1 A male and a female bobcat meet only to mate. About 10 weeks after mating, the female gives birth to a litter of 2—4 kittens in her den, usually a cave or a gap in the rocks.

2 The kittens are tiny, blind, and helpless. Their eyes open after 10 days, and they suckle milk from their mother for 2 months.

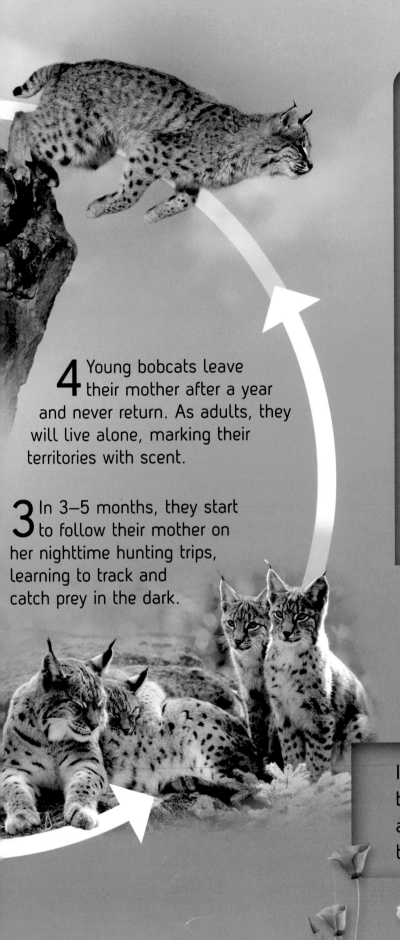

4 Young bobcats leave their mother after a year and never return. As adults, they will live alone, marking their territories with scent.

3 In 3–5 months, they start to follow their mother on her nighttime hunting trips, learning to track and catch prey in the dark.

Did you know?

Tufts of hair on the ear tips pick up tiny vibrations and help the bobcat hear the slightest sound.

The bobcat is named after its stubby, black-tipped tail that looks as if it has been cut, or "bobbed."

They have five toes on each foot, but one is raised and does not show on their tracks. The claws slide in when not in use.

It is not known for certain, but bobcats seem to live for about 12 years. Few animals threaten them as adults.

A Kalahari Desert food web

This book follows some desert food chains. Most animals eat more than one food, so they are part of many food chains. There are a lot of food chains in the desert, and they link up like a map to make a food web.

eagle

jackal

meerkat

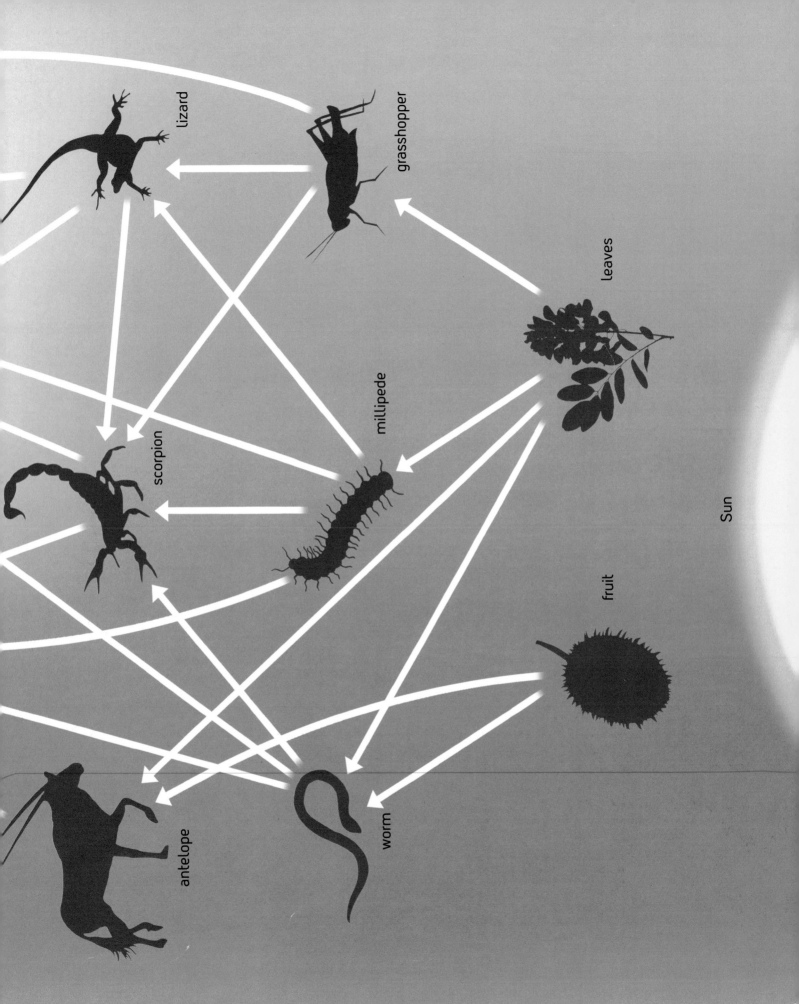

Glossary

ANTENNAE
A pair of feelers on an insect's head.

BROOD
A family of young animals, especially of birds, that all hatch at the same time.

BURROW
A hole or tunnel in the ground where an animal lives.

CANINE TEETH
Special long, pointed teeth used for piercing and gripping food.

COLONY
A group of the same kinds of animals that live together.

CONSUMER
A living thing that survives by eating other living things.

DEN
A wild animal's home.

EXOSKELETON
The hard layer on the outside of an insect's body. Spiders and millipedes also have exoskeletons.

HATCHLING
An animal just born from its egg.

HIBERNATE
When an animal rests through the winter.

LITTER
A group of baby animals born to the same mother.

MATE
When a male and female animal reproduce. For some animals, there is a particular time each year when they mate and this is called the "mating season."

MOLAR TEETH
Wide, flat teeth used for grinding food.

MOLT
When an animal gets rid of the outside of its body. This is also called shedding.

MOUND
A large pile of earth created by termites and used as their nest.

NYMPH
A young insect that is not yet fully grown and has no wings.

PINCERS
Grippers that scorpions use to hold prey.

PLUMAGE
A bird's feathers.

PREDATOR
An animal that kills and eats other animals.

PREY
An animal hunted by a predator.

PRODUCER
A living thing, such as a plant, that makes its own food using the energy of the sun.

SAC
A bag for holding eggs.

SCAVENGE
To search for and eat dead animals.

SEGMENT
A small part of the body.

SUCKLE
When a baby animal drinks milk from its mother.

SWARM
A large group of flying insects.

TERRITORY
An area of land where one animal or group of animals lives and hunts.

VENOM
A poisonous liquid injected by an animal to kill its prey.

VENOMOUS
Carrying venom.

YOLK
The nutrients inside an egg that feed a new baby animal.

These websites have information about deserts or their animals—or both!

- desertmuseum.org
- facts-about.org.uk/facts-about-the-desert.htm
- http://environment.nationalgeographic.com/environment/habitats/desert-profile/
- idahoptv.org/dialogue4kids/season3/desert/animals.cfm
- mojavedesert.net
- sandiegozoo.org/animalbytes/e-desert.html
- vtaide.com/png/foodchains.htm

Index